BUYING AND SELLING

A HOME

AMID COVID-19

A PERSONAL ACCOUNT

BUYING AND SELLING

A HOME

AMID COVID-19

A PERSONAL ACCOUNT

SYDELL A. JACKSON

Editorial Midwife Publishing

ORDERING INFORMATION

Quantity sales. On quantity purchases by corporations, associations, and others—orders by trade bookstores and wholesalers, contact Sydell Jackson at anayaru@bellsouth.net.

EDITORIAL SERVICES

Lita P. Ward, the Editorial Midwife
LPW Editing & Consulting Services, LLC
www.litapward.com

Published in the United States of America

ISBN: 9798709815131

DEDICATION

This book is dedicated to my grandmother
Hattie Mae Jacobs, who spent long hours
sharing blessed memories with me.

To my sister Patricia Ann Jackson, who
convinced me to move "down south"
to obtain a better life.

To my uncle James Warren, who continually
encouraged me all my life.

To my baby sister Pamela Marie Jackson, who
left this earth too soon.

FOREWORD

Have you ever been around someone who is somewhat quiet but always tuned in? Meet (Missionary) Sydell A. Jackson.

Proverbs 19:20-21 says, "Listen to advice and accept discipline, and at the end, you will be counted among the wise. Many are the plans in a person's heart, but it is the Lord's purpose that prevails.

As a kid, I was impressed with Sydell, who was a middle child in her family like me. She was a good student and an excellent reader. I purposed that I would learn to read as well and expressively as she did. I'm grateful for her example and inspiration to this day.

Sydell has been faithful to her calling as an ordained Missionary since the early 80's. Serving alongside her on many missionary assignments, I've witnessed how the Lord uses her and her gifts to be a blessing and bring healing to others.

Well, my best friend is actually from Never, Never Land; she never smoked, never drank, never did drugs, never backed down from a challenge that made sense to her. When housing was not affordable in Boston, where she grew up, she moved her family to Georgia. Her faith, hard work, and tenacious attitude allowed her to raise three beautiful daughters, obtain two degrees and purchase four houses. Through her experiences, she has been able to share her learnings and wisdom.

As well as being inquisitive, fun and witty, God has blessed Sydell with the gift of discernment. In the midst of an unclear situation, her gift gives her the ability to see things for what they **really** are, not what we **want** them to be. The largest transaction most of us will ever make is the purchase of a home. The sale of Sydell's last house and the purchase of her new one had its challenges that brought many stressful moments. She overcame those challenges. Sydell shares her knowledge and experience in this book to help others overcome looming pitfalls and obstacles. You will be blessed and glad you took the time to receive the gift of her wisdom and experience.

Evangelist Sandra West
Community Revival & Outreach Ministries
Boston, MA

ACKNOWLEDGEMENTS

First, I give honor and glory to God, Who is the Author and Finisher of my faith.

To my beautiful baby girl Angela, who, as soon as the virus hit, sacrificed her bedroom while sleeping on the couch for two months. It was a joy being catered to by her and my grandchildren Anaya and Adarius. Thank you, Angela, for being the strong and insightful woman you have become.

To my mother, Sadie Mae Jackson instilled in her seven children a sense of respect and integrity. My mom, who turned 94 years young on November 18th, 2020, taught my one brother and five sisters the old school adage that children are to be seen and not heard.

To Ms. Ida, my mother-in-law in North Carolina, who, along with my sisters, Bootsie, Joyce, Gloria, and my brother Larry took me under her wing. We share a bond so strong that I liken us to the biblical relationship that existed between Naomi and Ruth.

To Chi Chi, my beautiful real estate agent and new found friend. Chi Chi not only helped me with the purchase of my new home, but she continually kept me updated during the entire process. She explained every step we took and educated me on the many steps necessary in making a successful purchase. Chi Chi is truly a warrior princess and is my humble angel in disguise.

To Joye (Taz) Turner, my friend of twenty years, who when I needed a "helping hand," graciously extended one without hesitation. Thank you, Taz, for always lending me your ear and for your unwavering confidence in me.

To Evangelist Sandra (Sankie) West, my friend of sixty years. Thank you for your fervent and effectual prayers and for reminding me that "the Lord will always allow his children to triumph." Thank you for continuing to be my prayer warrior all the way through.

To my good friend Roxyanne and my sister Nedra, who always took the time to lend a listening ear and inspiring me to keep the faith.

To Lita Ward, my gifted and insightful editor. Thank you for allowing me to be your client and sharing your technical expertise and sound, wise advice.

To all the people who were brought into my life during that six month period and were instrumental in assisting me in preparing two homes for buying and selling. God bless you all!

To Evangelist Sandra West, thank you for writing a beautiful and enlightening Foreword for my first book.

TABLE OF CONTENTS

CHAPTER ONE

MY DECISION TO MOVE

During the year 2018, I began to contemplate relocating. The quiet and friendly neighborhood that I lived in just wasn't the same. Many of the neighbors I knew had moved, and the homeowner's association that was once vibrant was no more. After many months of prayer and indecisiveness, I finally decided in the year 2019 that my 2,362 square foot single family home was getting to be too much for a retired single woman to maintain. The home consisted of eight rooms upstairs and a partially finished nine-room basement. I retired from a major company five years before, traveled some, and continued to be the mainstay for my family. I needed a change in my life, and one of those changes consisted of me down-sizing.

After reconnecting with my former husband and his family in North Carolina, my ex and I decided to reconcile. After much discussion, the idea of moving from Georgia to North Carolina began formulating. By the time the year 2020 rolled around, my mind was made up. I was putting the home that I had spent the last fifteen years in up for sale; March was to be the "magic month."

Through December, I began packing and depersonalizing the home by packing away family pictures and personal items. At the same time, my daughter Angela and my sister Nedra's daughter, Bambi, gifted us a cruise for our birthdays. My sister's birthday is February 11th, and mine is February 12th. We always try to celebrate together by taking a trip abroad. During the entire trip, my mind was totally made up. I wasn't taking another cruise as I was tired of traveling on an often overcrowded vessel. The first thing I was going to do was contact my real estate agent.

On March 2, 2020, I contacted the same real estate agent who helped me purchase my second home in 1997 and then helped me sell that same home in 2017, sold in twenty-one days. Faith, my agent and now a friend, officially put my house on the market. I left my furniture in the home for staging to assist with the sale, packed my car up with only the essentials, and headed further east to North Carolina. I was both excited and apprehensive about my decision but was confident that whatever path I chose, God would direct me in the right direction.

Fear thou not; for I am with thee: be not dismayed; for I am God: I will strengthen thee; yea, I will help thee; yea, I will uphold thee with the right hand of my righteousness.

Isaiah 41:10

CHAPTER TWO

DECIDING WHERE TO LIVE

Though I have been divorced from my husband for over ten years, I managed to maintain a warm and loving relationship with my elderly mother-in-law and his sisters through the years. I began visiting my extended family in North Carolina. Ms. Ann and I enjoyed our visits so much that we were determined not to allow any negative forces to interfere with our relationship. My ex was so happy to see that I held no remorseful feelings from a messy divorce. And also appeared to be happy to see me. He was so happy that we began discussing the possibility of reconciling and pursuing a long-distance relationship.

The year 2016 was when I began periodically making the drive from Georgia to North Carolina. A lot had transpired by the time I drove there on March 5, 2020, with the intention of becoming a citizen of North Carolina. My ex and I determined in only one week that this relationship was not meant to be. So, I drove on down the road to my mother-in-law's home and began re-evaluating my plans.

While trying to determine where I wanted to live, talk began surfacing about a fast-moving virus over-whelming the world that had begun in China. The virus, labeled the Coronovirus – 20, was already bringing countries worldwide to a standstill and was threatening to do the same to the United States. Stores and businesses began running out of essential items such as toilet paper, hand sanitizer, Clorox wipes, Lysol, and numerous other cleaning products. Eventually, buying food was becoming an issue. What is now known as the Coronavirus pandemic of 2020 had come to fruition, taking the entire world by storm. The housing market faced a lot of uncertainty in March, but because of low-interest rates and what seemed to be the desire for more space, the market was booming.

My mind was made up, I decided to head back to Georgia on March 20, 2020, two weeks after arriving in North Carolina. I felt that if I was going to be stranded somewhere since talk was running rampant about the world shutting down, I needed to be closer to my children. My daughter, Lauren, had already suggested I come home and offered her bedroom. I didn't want to return to my house because I didn't want to get re-attached to it and change my mind because of the present state of the worldwide pandemic that was taking place. I had fifteen years of memories invested and intended to sell it, virus or no virus. I hunkered down in Lauren's apartment along with her and two of my grandchildren to shelter-in-place while the government continued to try to figure out what was going on.

But seek ye first the kingdom of God, and his righteousness, and all these things shall be added unto you.

Matthew 6:33

CHAPTER THREE
WHAT IS COVID-19?

Covid-19 is caused by a coronavirus called SARS-CoV2, according to the Center of Disease Control. The virus's main targets are older adults and people with underlying medical conditions such as heart or lung disease or diabetes. The virus was identified as far back as December in Wuhan, China, and is now being spread worldwide. Government officials in the United States did not make the American people aware of the virus until the middle of March.

The United States experienced a major attack of an infection 108 years when, in 1918 – 1919, a pandemic caused by an H1N1 virus with genes of avian (relating to birds) origin spread through Europe and the United States. It was estimated that about 500 million people or a third of the world's population became infected with the virus that became known as the "bird flu." The number of deaths was estimated to be at least 50 million worldwide, with about 675,000 deaths occurring in the United States. Eleven years later, in April 2009, the swine flu pandemic attack was caused by influenza A (H1N1). The quickly spreading virus affected children and adults over 65 who lacked immunity to H1N1. The estimated number of deaths from this virus was 12,469 in the United States. After administering a newly approved H1N1 vaccine to select Americans, the World Health Organization (WHO) declared an end to the pandemic on August 10, 2010.

I "sheltered in place" along with the rest of the world, only making the occasional trip to the grocery store when necessary. The state of Georgia began to re-open in April under the direction of our governor. After literally being confined to one bedroom in a small apartment for the past five weeks, I had more than enough time to contemplate my next move. I went online and began searching for homes for rent and for sale. I composed a shortlist of homes and asked my daughter if she would venture out with me to view the houses I found. My quest began.

My daughter Lauren and I went to the list of the five properties I found, at which time I made two important decisions. I was not going to rent, and I was going to purchase another house. Having been retired for the past six years and my only income from my pension and social security benefits, I knew that buying a home while I was still selling a home would be a challenge. I also knew that having a substantial bank account and credit score would "get my foot in the door," and I was right. My unwavering faith in God to provide for all my needs was another determining factor for me.

At this point, I made another decision. I needed professional help to have access to the inventory of homes in the area I was looking into and navigate the housing market during the pandemic. Because my real estate agent assisting me in selling my home seemed to be overwhelmed, I decided to incorporate another real estate agent for assistance in buying a home. I expressed interest online in a property Lauren and I had looked at. Before I knew it, a flurry of agents began texting and emailing me offering to help. I attempted to contact the six agents who had reached out to me, and only two returned my calls. My strategy was to reach out to the two who had at least returned my call, and whoever returned my call first was the one I would go with. That decision turned out to be one of the best decisions I could have made.

Now faith is the substance of things hoped for, the evidence of things not seen.

Hebrews 11: 1

CHAPTER FOUR
THE PROCESS

I was to find out that China possessed the rare traits of a real estate agent, passion and accountability, called me immediately. I mentioned to China that I was not only looking to purchase a home but that I was in the process of selling my existing home. Being a person of integrity, China asked me why I could not allow the agent I was working with on my home's sale to handle a new purchase. I mentioned that when I brought the subject to my present agent about my interest in purchasing a home, she didn't express interest.

On the drive back to Georgia, on March 20, 2020, my buying agent called to inform me that a couple who was relocating from the north to the south was interested in my property. This is the time when the world had just been informed about the coronavirus. I didn't hear from my agent again until six weeks later when I called to see what the status was, at which time she informed me that the couple had changed their mind. Due to the virus, they were not sure about how their income situation would play out. I was surprised that there had been no communication or follow-up and still would not have found out had I not called. I voiced my concern to my agent, who told me that she had been working hard on this and asked me to be patient. She asked that I please let her do her job.

As defined by the Cambridge Dictionary, a real estate agent is a person whose business arranges the selling, buying, or renting of houses, land, offices, or buildings for their owners. While this career can be appealing and offers challenges or opportunities, an agent's skill set needs to be constantly honed to keep up with the current market. From personal experience, I was finding, as with all aspects of life where communication is an important entity, that working with the agent

I had chosen to sell my house would be a challenge.

I had a lot of confidence in my real estate agent, Faith, from past experience. In the year 1996, Faith had helped me to find and purchase a home. The housing market at that time was decidedly different than it is now. There was plenty of inventory, and the purchasing process was easy and seamless.

Twenty years later, in the year 2017, Faith helped me sell the same house that she sold me those many years ago. Faith was able to sell that house in record time, twenty-one days. Except for signing the necessary documents online, I didn't have much involvement. I was given a closing date and time, went to the lawyer's office, signed the papers, received a check, and was done.

When I decided to sell my present home, there was no question in my mind that I would hire Faith. Along with this decision came the realization that not only had the housing market changed but so had my friend. Through the entire process of selling my home, I had to force communication.

I changed my mind multiple times on what to do about the house. I believed that the house would sell because the interest was definitely there. Still, I began to wonder if my expectations of selling it during a virus were unrealistic. The multiple changes and adjustments that my agent was making without my knowledge were becoming frustrating. I became so overwhelmed that I contemplated refinancing or renting it out.

Immersing myself in my house hunting efforts, which entailed my new found agent and friend, China, gave me plenty to think about. We embarked on our adventure, searching for a home during a pandemic. The first step was finding a lender who could assist me with obtaining a loan. That also meant getting pre-approved, which became a challenge in itself. I assumed that having a healthy bank account and an excellent credit score should be enough for any lender to not see giving me a loan as a risk. China introduced me to Frank, the lender. He didn't foresee any problems after checking my score and seemed very anxious to secure a loan. Frank was confident that we would make it work, so confident that he sent me the pre-approval letter from his bank for the loan. China and I "hit the ground running;" we were averaging two to three houses a day and found a possible prospect on our third trip out. China informed Frank that we may have found a house.

When reviewing a mortgage application, the lender's role is looking for overall positive credit history, a low amount of debt, and steady income, among other factors. When I began the loan process with Frank, we were in contact with each other almost every day. I copied, scanned, and rescanned so many documents, I felt I was working a part-time job. I noticed that I was calling Frank and not receiving any return calls. On one of these occasions, I tried calling, and my call was dismissed. I expressed my concern to

China, who interceded and contacted Frank. We found out that the lender could not assist me because I still owned my other home and that my ability to obtain a loan would have to be contingent on my present home's sale. Frank appeared to have decided to simply ignore my calls and avoid me. Once again, I noticed that the element of communication was not as important as it used to be.

China managed to find another lender, Arnold, who, like the first lender, viewed my credit score and felt his company could help me obtain a loan. The difference between Arnold and Frank was that Arnold was not afraid to confront me with the facts. We ran into the same situation as I did with the first lender; I still owned a home that I was paying a mortgage on. Arnold quickly looked for different solutions to solve the problem, my not being employed and having a home still on the market.

Having been through the drill before, I knew what was expected of me. Sometimes I felt like my integrity was being scrutinized. I spent a lot of time proving my income was legitimate even though I was sending and resending bank and IRA statements. Though I knew everything was true and above board, I couldn't get around the fact that my home had not sold yet. Confident that I could pay all of my bills and afford to pay another mortgage as long as I stayed within my price range, I had to get creative.

Meanwhile, my buying agent found another buyer for my home; this was prospect number two. We made it all the way to signing a contract, the buyer was pre-approved and set a closing date for June. We didn't make it to closing as the buyer changed her mind experiencing what is called "buyer's remorse," and the search continued.

China and I continued to search for a home for me. The obstacle we were coming up against was though the coronavirus was gripping the world, it was not affecting the housing market. Interest rates were remaining low, and people were taking advantage of this fact. The lack of inventory was great, and every house I expressed interest in was literally snatched from under me. Bidding wars were occurring left and right. The right bid and timing are everything in the real estate world.

My buying agent found another interested prospect for my home; this would be prospect number three. The contract was signed, the buyer was pre-approved, and the closing date was set for June 21st. The buyer ordered an inspection to be done on the home. During the inspection process, the inspector listed that there was possibly mold in the basement. Having young children who had respiratory issues, the buyer changed her mind about purchasing the home. Again, the house was put back on the market.

At the same time, my selling agent and I found just the right home for me. The house was in total disarray but was in just the right area I was interested in and was exactly the right size I was looking for. In 2007, the house had good bones, and I knew I could bring it back to its original glory. Since I had about five homes snatched from under me, China and I went in with a strategy to ensure that I would get this house! We submitted a bid slightly over the selling price and got the contract on April 27, 2020.

My loan had made it to the underwriting stage, whose role is to carefully scrutinize the application. The underwriting department helps the lender decide whether you will get a loan approval and work with you to make sure that you submit all your paperwork. The underwriter will ensure that you don't close on a mortgage that you cannot afford. This process should take at least 30 days or more. I had to go the extra mile in that I had to have my financial advisor submit a letter reporting my income. Plus, I had to pay off two small balances to loans to meet the 50% debt to income ratio. That entailed my paying the loans off, contacting the companies and obtaining letters from them proving that I had paid the loans off and sent this information to the underwriters.

While still waiting to get an okay on the loan, I ordered an inspection for the home I was purchasing. The 106-page report revealed multiple issues that needed to be addressed. My agent went back to the seller's agent to negotiate reducing the house price due to the many issues. The choices were making the necessary repairs or money coming off the sale price; we chose the latter. The sellers agreed to take money off the sale price, which meant we were back in business and the appraisal was ordered.

The real estate appraiser's role is to help their clients systematically determine the market value of a property, which is one of the first steps in any real estate transaction, whether you are a buyer, seller, lender, or other interested party. The house was appraised "as is"; the only step was waiting for the underwriting department to give the okay to proceed with the sale. I received the "clear to close" with the closing date set for May

27, 2020, thirty days after finding the property. In the real estate world, closing dates are not "set in stone," which applied to my closing. The closing date was moved to May 29, 2020, because a document was not signed on time. Finally, a little more than a month after going house hunting during the pandemic and finding a property, I received my papers and keys to my new home.

I will lift up mine eyes unto the hills, from whence cometh my help. My help cometh from the Lord, which made heaven and earth.

Psalms 121: 1-2

CHAPTER FIVE
MY NEW HOME ADVENTURE

I began meeting with contractors to make plans for an entire home renovation. The whole interior needed to be painted, floors had to be ripped up, and new carpet and floors had to be installed. Closet doors and window screens had to be replaced throughout the entire house. I wasn't able to move in until June 5, 2020, a week after I closed.

A veteran, who had previously viewed the house that I was still selling about three times, was still interested in purchasing it; this would be prospect number four. Another inspection was ordered for the home. As with everything else, different home inspectors focus on different items. This was the second inspection that was to be conducted on this home, and I didn't want the same issues from the first inspection to come up. The real estate agent for the prospective buyer ordered another inspection that I had to stop so I could be allowed to make corrections. I had to pull my "owner's rights" card to stop this inspection from proceeding. I did and corrected every item from the first inspection.

Totally different items were noted on the second inspection. I had already made the necessary repairs from the first inspection and didn't expect too many issues. The inspector managed to find some issues that needed to be addressed. I decided that I was unwilling to invest more money on repairs and would rather deduct a reasonable amount from the purchase price. Everyone agreed. Each time there are any changes to a contract, the contract must be edited and re-signed by all parties. The appraisal was then ordered and would take place within the week.

Because the interested party was a veteran, he applied through the Veteran Administration (VA) loan program. The VA loan program was created to help open doors of homeownership to more veterans, military members, and their families. There is a broad criterion that VA backed homes must be measured against known as "Minimum Property Requirements," or MPRs. The home has to meet the VA's appraisal guidelines and lender requirements. The VA appraisal helps veterans and service members purchase safe, sanitary, structurally sound, and appropriately valued homes.

Through my entire venture with Faith, our problem has continued to be the fact that she would not communicate with me. In other words, she would not "keep me in the loop." But continues to tell me that when she knew something, I would. All the while, I found out later, she had many plans formulated regarding my property.

Three weeks later, I had not heard anything about how the appraisal went and had not heard anything from my agent, so I contacted her. From recently purchasing a house myself, I knew that covid or no covid, an appraisal should not take three weeks. My agent checked the status by contacting the lender. At that time, we found out that the prospective buyer had filled out his financial information incorrectly on the application and that underwriting was checking into it. In the meantime, another interested party submitted a contract for the purchase of my home; this would be prospect number five.

On July 21, 2020, my real estate agent emailed me another purchase and sale agreement from the interested party with a closing date of August 31, 2020. This meant that the house was going to need to be inspected and appraised again.

Again, different items were noted on the third inspection. The interested buyer was very adamant about purchasing the home and wanted every issue addressed at my expense. At this point in my making the repairs, the difference was that most of the changes appeared to be cosmetic. These changes included painting the front door a different color, repairing and painting the large deck attached to the home, and replacing the back door that led to the patio. I felt like I was doing a home renovation and was getting a little frustrated. I had already spent money addressing issues from the last two inspection reports.

I informed my agent that she would have to be responsible for finding someone to do the work, and I needed to agree with the price. My agent, sensing my frustration, agreed with my terms, found a contractor who submitted a reasonable proposal. My agent also agreed to pay out of pocket for any expenses incurred and surpassed the price I agreed to. This kind gesture helped to relieve some of the pressure I was feeling.

At the same time, the appraisal was being conducted, the appraiser was finding different issues with the house that they felt needed to be addressed before the final sale. Another appointment needed to be scheduled for a second appraisal after all the documented repairs were made. Since the appraiser and FHA had to inspect the property again, the closing date was changed to September 3, 2020, at 2:00 to ensure that all of the necessary documents were processed. At this time, I found out that the buyers were investors because the investor's funds had not reached the lawyer's office.

The property was appraised for a lower price than the original price by $12,000. This was no surprise to me, and I understood that investing what I had would still yield a reasonable profit. We were on our last leg and needed that final push to reach home.

For we walk by faith and not by sight.
2 Corinthians 5:7

CHAPTER SIX
TO CLOSE OR NOT TO CLOSE

On September 3rd, 2020, I prepared to make the journey to downtown Atlanta, where the lawyer's office was located. I had arranged for my new best friend, China, to take me to the lawyer's office. I haven't driven in the downtown Atlanta area in years, and China graciously offered to take me to my closing. I received a phone call at 12:45pm from Faith informing me that the closing time had been changed from 2:00pm to 4:00pm because the lawyer's office experienced a computer glitch. China and I decided to make it through the hustle and bustle of navigating the Atlanta traffic and have lunch while waiting.

At 3:00pm, while China and I were enjoying our meal outside of the famous take out place, The Varsity, I received a call from Cindy from the lawyer's office advising me that we would not be able to conduct the closing at 4:00pm; the office had not received the "clear to close" document. Cindy scheduled an in-home signing for my convenience to be conducted the next day, Friday, September 4th, at 7:00pm. China and I proceeded to make the hour-long drive back to my home in Covington.

Friday seemed to drag, and I did everything that I could to stay busy, even managing to run out and take care of a few errands. I received a call from Cindy at 5:32pm to inform me that we would have to re-schedule the closing once again. The lawyer's office was supposed to submit all of the paperwork three hours before the signing occurred to gain access to them. The lawyers missed the three-hour window; therefore, Cindy and the investor re-scheduled. The appointment to come to my home was changed to Tuesday, September 8th at 3:00pm because September 7th was a holiday.

On Tuesday, September at 4:00pm, all essential parties converged on my home to sign all of the necessary documents. In an hour's time, with all documents signed, we could all breathe a sigh of relief.

But my God will supply all your needs according to his riches in glory by Christ Jesus.

Philippians 4:19

CHAPTER SEVEN
LESSONS LEARNED

This has been a year like no other that the world has ever known. When I put my home on the market almost a year ago, little did I know that I would be confronted with so many challenges beginning with one of the most horrific viruses' to hit the nation in 102 years. Buying and selling a house during the coronavirus has taught me many lessons about life that I thought I already knew.

The year 2020 saw me returning from a cruise to Mexico to battling a virus with the rest of the world. I should have known something was terribly wrong when the cruise line began sending out announcements that we would not have to be concerned about cruising with people from China. When I got off the bus that took us from the airport to Biscayne Boulevard and saw a busload of Asians, some of them wearing masks,

I definitely had no clue that there was a hint of a bigger problem occurring. The rumor that began circulating as time went by was that cruise ships unknown to anyone were floating petri dishes during that time.

I have learned to value every precious moment that the Lord has blessed me with. Stay informed about what is happening globally, and be compassionate and patient about other people's situations.

Buying a home in the year 2004 was a bit easier than buying a home in 2020. I was not only navigating the housing market during the virus issue, but I was confronted with major bidding wars. The interest rates had plummeted, and people were relocating and buying larger homes to obtain more space. I missed out on seven opportunities by outbids; that was frustrating. Not having a "defeated" attitude and putting all my faith and trust in God, I believed that what was meant for me would be.

The competitive world of real estate is not for the faint-hearted. Building your hopes up just to be disappointed by another setback is the norm. Through the entire process, emotions go up and down as if being on a continual roller coaster ride. Timing is everything, and freedom and plenty of energy are essential. For six months, my world consisted of contracts, inspections, appraisals, real-estate sales, repairs, and renovations. Though it was a lot of work mentally, emotionally, and physically, I made many new friends and even managed to lose twenty pounds.

With each ending comes a new beginning, and I have learned through this entire journey that the shortest way may not always be the best way. Sometimes God allows us to take the longer route in life to be better prepared for the journey ahead. When things don't seem to happen quickly enough, we can trust in God, the one who leads and guides us. After finally being able to exhale, I can truly testify that my actions and decisions were guided by the Spirit of God.

Trust in the Lord with all thine heart; and lean not unto thine own understanding. In all thy ways acknowledge him, and he shall direct thy paths.

Proverbs 3:5-6